Succeed as a musician without sacrificing your faith

STUDY GUIDE

ALLEN C. PAUL

# God and Gigs: Study Guide

Copyright © 2016 by Allen C. Paul

All rights reserved. This book or any portion thereof may not be reproduced or used in any manner whatsoever without the express written permission of the publisher except for the use of brief quotations in a book review.

Printed in the United States of America
First Printing, 2016
ISBN 978-0-9972703-2-7
www.GodandGigs.com

# CONTENTS

How To Use This Study Guide ..................................................... 4

Introduction ........................................................................ 6

Chapter One: Stay Connected to the Church ................................. 9

Chapter Two: Stay Connected to your Spouse ............................. 14

Chapter Three: Stay Connected to your Children ......................... 18

Chapter Four: Stay Connected to God ........................................ 22

Chapter Five: Establish your Priorities ...................................... 25

Chapter Six: Respect the Business ............................................ 29

Chapter Seven: Visualizing your Goals ...................................... 33

Chapter Eight: Invest in your Skill ............................................ 37

Chapter Nine: Challenge yourself to Grow ................................. 41

Chapter Ten: Evangelize through your Gift ................................ 45

The Follow Through: ............................................................. 48

Complete List Of Scripture References ..................................... 55

# How to use this Study Guide

As you read *God and Gigs: Succeed as a Musician without Sacrificing your Faith*, you'll find several concepts in the book that can change and improve your life. This study guide will help you think about your artistic career, identify areas in which you can improve, and follow through with your commitments. It can be used individually or as a small group study among artists, musicians and creatives.

To get the most out of this guide, do each exercise with three accompanying resources: your *God and Gigs* book, a Bible to reference the scripture passages, and a journal to write your reflections. Don't merely read the questions; think deeply about your responses. As you go through the guide, mark passages that relate directly to your situations and review them often. I highly suggest using good old fashioned handwriting for your responses. People tend to think differently and more deeply when we write versus when we type.

The Follow-Through Section of this Guide is intended to be filled out 2 – 3 weeks AFTER you have completed each section. Don't do it before the time has passed! Any new behavior we attempt takes 21 days to become a habit. Once you have made strides in each of the 7 SERVICE steps, go to the Follow Through and note the positive changes you've made as a fulfilled and faithful artist. You'll find these principles will make a bigger impact on your life if you follow through the right way.

Think, grow and remember to keep God in the center of your artistic career.

# Introduction

## Questions for Further Discussion:

1. Have you ever sensed a conflict between your faith and your career? When did it happen? How did it make you feel?

_____
_____
_____
_____
_____
_____

2. Have you ever had to defend your career choice? If so, how did you respond?

_____
_____
_____
_____
_____
_____

3. What part of Allen's story did you most identify with?
_____
_____
_____
_____
_____
_____

4. The S.E.R.V.I.C.E. steps lay out a plan for keeping your faith intact as you work in the broader music industry. **They are:**

    **S**tay Connected
    **E**stablish your Priorities
    **R**espect the Business
    **V**isualize your Goals
    **I**nvest in Your Skill
    **C**hallenge Yourself to Grow
    **E**vangelize through your Gift

In what areas do you need to grow? In what areas are you more confident?

_____
_____
_____
_____
_____
_____
_____

## Recommended Bible Reading

Nehemiah 13:7-14
1 Peter 2:9
2 Chronicles 23:18

## Action Steps:

Begin a journal in which you'll review your attitudes, routines and goals as you go through the book.

# Chapter One

## Stay Connected to Church

## Questions for Further Discussion:

Why is joining a church viewed negatively by musicians? Have you ever been discouraged from connecting with a church by another musician? What was their rationale?

_____
_____
_____
_____
_____
_____

If you aren't a member of a church, what factors have kept you from joining one?

_____
_____
_____
_____
_____
_____
_____

Think about your experiences in church and local ministries. Have they been generally positive or negative? What factors contributed to those experiences?

_____
_____
_____
_____
_____
_____
_____

Do you have a group of artists with whom you can share your struggles? If not, where could you begin to build this circle of trusted peers?

_____
_____
_____
_____
_____

Do you have relationships in your church that are unrelated to musical duties or worship services? If so, how can you improve and strengthen them? If you don't have any, what ministries could you join that fit your personality and interests?

_____
_____
_____
_____
_____

Do you have relationships in your church that are unrelated to musical duties or worship services? If so, how can you improve and strengthen them?

_____
_____
_____
_____
_____
_____

## Recommended Bible Reading:

Psalms 92:13
Ecclesiastes 4:9-12
Hebrews 10:24-25

## Action Steps:

1. If you are a member of a church, evaluate your connections with the people and ministries. If they aren't strong and vibrant, consider a one month trial period during which you will get more involved.

2. If you aren't a member of a church, read the heading "What To Look For In A Church" and explore ministries in your area that fit the criteria listed.
3. Think about your closest artistic relationships. Do you have friends that you can trust and confide in? If not, list 5 people that could be a part of your accountability partnership.

# Chapter Two

## Stay Connected to your Spouse

Questions for Further Discussion:

Is a romantic relationship with a musician different than with someone in another profession? Why or why not?

_____
_____
_____
_____
_____
_____

Can a healthy marriage and a healthy career co-exist? If it can, what factors make this possible?

_____
_____

If you are married, what steps are you taking to reinforce and strengthen your relationship? Have you planned strategically how you'll do this?

If you're not married and are actively pursuing a relationship, what factors in your life contribute to your readiness for marriage? What factors are a hindrance?

What aspects of your career may need to be adjusted in order to make a relationship work?

_____
_____
_____
_____
_____
_____

## Recommended Bible Reading:

Ephesians 5:22-33
1 Thessalonians 4:2 – 7

## Action Steps:

1. If you are married, plan a date night that isn't music-related. Make a point not to go to venues that you associate with your music career.
2. Sit down with your spouse and discuss how your career has positively impacted your relationship. Then list the ways that your career has created struggle. Discuss ways

to increase the positive effects and diminish the negative effects so that you are both united on your future decisions.
3. If you're in a committed relationship or are seeking one, make a list of possible conflicts between your career and relationship. Think creatively about how you can balance the needs of your career while prioritizing the needs of your significant other.

# Chapter Three

## Stay Connected to your Children

Questions for Further Discussion:

Where you raised in a musical family? If so, how did your experience affect your approach to your career? If not, how did your family support your aspirations?

_____
_____
_____
_____
_____
_____

The book mentions six steps to successful parenting as a performing artist. Which step do you feel you need to work on the most? (If you do not have children, which step do you think you would struggle with the most?)

Is parenting as a musician harder than parenting in other professions? Why or why not?

In what ways do children brought up in a musical household differ from those that are not?

What are the benefits and the negatives of having a family that is heavily involved in the arts?

_____
_____
_____
_____
_____
_____

## Recommended Bible Reading:

Psalms 127:3
Luke 9:25
Proverbs 22:6

## Action Steps:

1. If you are a parent, take inventory of how many one-on-one moments you have with your children. If they aren't happening frequently, adjust your work / church schedule and dedicate some time to building your relationships with your children.

2. If you have older children (teens), talk to them about your career and why you make certain sacrifices. Then ask them about their dreams and goals so you can help them find paths to achieving them.
3. If you are not a parent, look for opportunities to mentor and help young children through arts programs and outreach. Use these opportunities to share your experiences and pass them on to the next generation of musicians.

# Chapter Four

## Stay Connected to God

### Questions for Further Discussion:

Answer the three opening questions in Chapter 4 and rate your answer on a scale of one to five.
(1 – never, 5 – always)

Do I consistently study the Bible?  Y  N
How often?  1  2  3  4  5

Do I have set devotional times and keep them?  Y  N
How often? 1 2 3 4 5

Do I pray regularly? Y  N
How often? 1 2 3 4 5

Do you ever feel awkward or unwilling to pray in certain situations? Do you feel God is less likely to hear your prayers because of your profession? Why or why not?

_____
_____
_____
_____
_____

How has Bible reading impacted your everyday life? If you don't read your Bible regularly, what would help you become more consistent?

_____
_____
_____
_____
_____

Is your faith ever mentioned or discussed at your public performances? When does it usually happen? If the comments are negative, how do you deal with them?

_____
_____

_____

_____

_____

## Recommended Bible Reading:

James 5:13-18
Matthew 6:33
Psalms 37:4
Matthew 5:14 – 16

## Action Steps:

1. If you don't have a set devotional / Bible reading time, commit to keeping one for 21 days. (Consider The God and Gigs 21 day devotional)
2. Pick a scripture verse relating to music to memorize over the next week. Psalms has several verses that mention music. Quote that verse to yourself before and after your performances.

# Chapter Five

## Establish your Priorities

### Questions for Further Discussion:

Think about the past 30 days. What priorities have dominated your career choices and schedule? Are you happy with the choices you've made? Why or why not?

_____
_____
_____
_____
_____
_____

Think about times where you had to make a decision between two competing priorities. Which one won out? Why did you pick that one? Do you still think you made the right choice?

## Allen C. Paul

What motivates you most as an artist? What part of your craft makes you the happiest?

Do you consider yourself an amateur, semi-pro, or a professional?

If you feel that you want to move up to a professional level, what steps do you need to take? What aspects of being a professional artist scares you the most? If you are a professional, what has been the hardest part of maintaining your status?

_____
_____
_____
_____
_____
_____
_____

## Recommended Bible Reading:

Proverbs 29:15
Proverbs 11:14
Philippians 2:3-4
Habakkuk 2:2 (The Message)
Ephesians 3:22

## Action Steps:

1. Make a list of all the goals that you have for your musical or artistic career. Then pick one that you will focus on for 90 days. Make sure you schedule one task a day that pertains specifically to that goal.
2. If you could spend your time doing any particular musical activity without any financial restraints, what would it be? Write it down, then devise a plan to do that activity more often than any other.
3. If you want to increase your level of musicianship from amateur or semi-pro to professional, find a mentor or accountability partner that can advise you on your progress and remind you of your commitments as you pursue this goal.

# Chapter Six

## Respect the Business

## Questions for Further Discussion:

The three keys of professionalism are presentation, preparation, and punctuality. Which of these areas are you strongest in? Weakest in? How can you improve?

_____
_____
_____
_____
_____
_____

Think about a time when you faced a schedule conflict. Did it work out smoothly or were there problems? What could you have changed to make it work out better?

Have you ever been unprepared for a performance? What was the result? What was the response of the other musicians?

Have you ever had to break away from a long-term musical partnership or relationship? What was the result? Was the overall experience positive or negative? If negative, how could it have been handled differently?

## Recommended Bible Reading:

Matthew 5:38
James 4:1
Zechariah. 8:16
Psalms 73:16-17
Ephesians 6:10-11

## Action Steps:

1. Think about the three areas of professionalism, and write down three ways you can improve in your weakest area. For example, if your issue is punctuality, you could commit to arriving 10 min early, make lists of all needed materials the night before, and invest in a traffic / GPS app.
2. Think about relationships you have within your musical circle. If there is a negative or unhealthy career relationship, think of ways you can begin to build trust and restoration. If that is impossible, write down and plan a graceful and humble way to end the partnership without anger or bitterness.

ALLEN C. PAUL

Check your calendar and make a note of any schedule conflicts (or potential ones). Make a commitment to either eliminate potential conflicts, or notify the parties involved so that every party is able to adjust schedules and maintain their commitments.

# Chapter Seven

## Visualize your Goals

Questions for Further Discussion:

Do you have career goals that require more intentional planning? If so, what's stopped you from making those plans?

_____
_____
_____
_____
_____
_____

Have you written down a vision statement before? If so, was it specific, measurable, attainable, reality-based and time-sensitive? If not, which of these areas do you need to focus on when you write it?

_____
_____
_____
_____

Have you made your goals public, or do you keep them to yourself? What is the rationale behind your promotion or lack of it?

_____
_____
_____
_____

Do you fear a negative response to your promotional activities? Why or why not?

_____
_____
_____
_____

How do you support the visions of other artists in your area? If you don't currently do so, in what ways can you begin to help other artists achieve their goals?

_____
_____
_____
_____
_____
_____
_____

## Recommended Bible Reading:

Proverbs 29:15
Proverbs 11:14
Philippians 2:3-4
Habakkuk 2:2 (The Message)
Ephesians 3:22

## Action Steps:

1. Write your vision statement for your career, if you have not already. Make sure your vision contains S.M.A.R.T. characteristics (Specific, Measurable, Attainable, Results – based, and Time – Sensitive). If you have a vision statement, consider how you've implemented your stated goals during the last 90 days. Are you operating in line with your current vision? If not, either change your activities to align with your vision, or revise your vision statement to more accurately reflect your goals.
2. Develop an 'elevator pitch', a single statement or phrase that defines your musical brand or approach. Make sure this phrase helps a potential client or buyer to understand you and your unique sound. Then use this pitch in your promotional activities.
3. Find at least 3 other artists and projects that you believe in and can support. Then make those supporting those artists and projects a regular part of your schedule and promotional activity. Actively find ways that you can collaborate with these artists to make each of your projects more effective and visible to your common audiences.

# Chapter Eight

## Invest in Your Skill

## Questions for Further Discussion:

Do you have a track record of investing back into your career? If so, what tangible results have come from your efforts?

_____
_____
_____
_____
_____
_____

Do you plan ahead for major equipment purchases, or do you simply buy things when you think you need them? Which of these methods is more effective?

_____
_____
_____
_____
_____
_____

Are your promotional products (business cards, websites, etc.) consistently of high quality? If so, how have you used them to your advantage? If not, what can you do to develop these materials?

_____
_____
_____
_____
_____
_____

How much time do you regularly invest into practice and continued musical education? In what ways can you use this time more effectively and become more proficient?

_____
_____
_____
_____
_____
_____
_____

## Recommended Bible Reading:

Matt 25:14-29
Luke 14:28 – 31
Proverbs 21:5
Ecclesiastes 11:2

## Action Steps:

1. Develop a systematic investment plan for purchasing or updating your equipment. Options could include saving a percentage of every performance check for future investments in gear, doing a quarterly inventory, selling old or outdated equipment, etc.
2. Choose at least one area of your branding to upgrade or improve, whether it be social media or other online imaging, business cards, flyers or other promotional materials. Make sure that you budget adequately for your upgrade by getting quotes from reputable sources.

Commit to improving your performance skill or artistic knowledge in at least one area of your career over the next six months. Set a benchmark that will indicate a measurable improvement in this area (a technique you have mastered, passing a test or class, completing a new online course) For great resources to help you set and achieve goals such as these, check out **GodandGigs.com**

# Chapter Nine

## Challenge Yourself to Grow

### Questions for Further Discussion:

What does true fulfillment mean to an artist? What does it mean to you? Is it possible to find it in your career alone?

_____
_____
_____
_____
_____
_____

Have you ever felt what Darlene Zschech calls "emotional fervor" after a performance, when you slipped from a performance 'high' to feeling depressed and empty? How did you deal with these feelings? What strategies could you use to overcome or avoid the downturn in your emotions?

_____
_____
_____
_____
_____
_____

What activities do you value most outside of your artistic life? If your talent or gift was removed, could you find your purpose in these other areas?

_____
_____
_____
_____
_____
_____

How have you pushed yourself outside of your comfort zone in your creative pursuits? If you haven't, what types of activities would challenge you to grow?

_____
_____
_____

## Recommended Bible Reading:

Amos 5:18-24
2 Corinthians 3:17
Philippians 3:10 -14
1 Corinthians 13:1 -7

## Action Steps:

1. Pick at least one non-artistic discipline or hobby to develop in your spare time. If you already have a non-musical passion, work at intentionally developing it to a higher level.
2. In your journal, write down your feelings before and after your performances. Evaluate whether you are maintaining a sense of emotional balance, or if you have a pattern of tying your emotions to the quality of your performances.
3. Pick a musical or artistic area (for example, a new instrument, a different style of music, etc.) that is not in

your normal routine or performance regime, and commit to working on it for 1 month. After the month is over, you can choose to continue to work on it, or try a new one. Journal about your experiences.

# Chapter Ten

## Evangelize through your gift

### Questions for Further Discussion:

Do you sense that you stand out due to your faith or your moral choices when you perform outside of the church? How does that affect you? Have you ever felt pressure to compromise your beliefs in these environments?

_____
_____
_____
_____
_____
_____

How have you seen the power of a giving attitude in your relationships? Have you ever been tempted to give less of yourself because of worry or fear of rejection?

Have you ever shared your faith directly with another musician? What was the result? If not, how have you impacted your peers positively with your influence?

In what ways have you grown in your faith as you've navigated your career? How can you increase your influence and your ability to help others?

## Recommended Bible Reading:

Proverbs 18:16
Colossians 3:12-17
Numbers 18:6-7
Matthew 5:14-16

## Action Steps:

1. Intentionally determine ways that you can connect with and bless other artists in your circle of influence. Do this even if your efforts aren't noticed or appreciated.
2. Pray for the artists in and around your performances.
3. In the event that you can share the gospel with a friend, purpose in your heart to share your story honestly and humbly. Jesus always begun his conversations with outsiders by starting from where they were. He never started with facts or scriptures. In the same way, pray and prepare to share your faith in a way that reveals God's heart of love.

# The Follow Through:

What Changed?
(DON'T FILL OUT THIS SECTION TIL AT LEAST TWO WEEKS AFTER FINISHING THE BOOK / GUIDE)

_____
_____
_____
_____
_____
_____
_____

## Staying Connected:

I used to…

_____
_____
_____

_____
_____
_____

Now I...

_____
_____
_____
_____
_____
_____


## Establish your Priorities:

I used to...

_____
_____
_____
_____
_____
_____

Allen C. Paul

Now I...

_____
_____
_____
_____
_____
_____

## Respect the Business:

I used to...

_____
_____
_____
_____
_____
_____

Now I...

_____
_____
_____
_____

_____
_____
_____

## Visualize your Goals:

I used to…

_____
_____
_____
_____
_____
_____

Now I…

_____
_____
_____
_____
_____
_____

## Invest in your Skill:

I used to…

_____
_____
_____
_____
_____
_____

Now I…

_____
_____
_____
_____
_____
_____

## Challenge Yourself to Grow:

I used to…

_____
_____
_____
_____

_____
_____
_____

Now I…
_____
_____
_____
_____
_____


## Evangelize through your Gift:
I used to…
_____
_____
_____
_____
_____
_____

ALLEN C. PAUL

Now I…

_____
_____
_____
_____
_____
_____
_____

~

# Complete List of Scripture References

All scriptures taken from NIV unless otherwise noted

| Chapter 1 | Chapter 3 | Psalms 37:4 |
|---|---|---|
| Neh 13:10 | 1 Thess 4:2-7 | Matt 5:14 |
| 1 Peter 2:9 | (NLT) | 2 Tim 3:16 |
| 2 Chronicles 23:18 | Psalm 127:3 (NASB) | (NLT) |
| Chapter 2 | Luke 9:25 | Chapter 5 |
| Ecc 4:12 (NLT) | Chapter 4 | Matt 6:21 |
| Gen 11:6 | James 5:16 | Isaiah 40:28-31 |
| Psalms 94:12 | 2 Kings 5:18-19 | Luke 14:28 (NLT) |
| Romans 12:18 | Col 3:22-23 | Chapter 6 |
| Heb 10:24-25 | James 1:17 | Matt 5:38 |
| Zec 8:16 | Matt 6:33 | Jas 4:1 |
| Psalms 73:16-17 | Eph 4:12 | |

| | |
|---|---|
| (NASB) | **Chapter 10** |
| Eph 6:10-11 | Prov 18:16 |
| **Chapter 7** | Col 3:17 |
| Prov 29:15 | Num 18:7 |
| Prov 11:14 | Matt 5:16 |
| Phil 2:3-4 | 2 Cor 4:7 |
| Hab 2:2 (The Message) | Gal 5:19 – 20 |
| | 2 Cor 5:18 |
| Eph 3:22 | |
| **Chapter 8** | |
| Matt 25:14-29 | |
| **Chapter 9** | |
| Matt 10:39 | |
| Amos 5:23 | |
| 2 Cor 3:17 | |
| Phil 3:10 | |
| 1 Cor 13:1 | |
| Isaiah 40:31 | |
| Rom 11:29 (God's Word) | |

# NOTES

# NOTES

# NOTES

# NOTES

# NOTES

# NOTES

For More Information, Encouragement and Inspiration, visit

## GodandGigs.com

Sign up for our mailing list

## Godandgigs.com/signup

Buy the Book- God and Gigs: Succeed as a Musician without Sacrificing your Faith

## GodandGigsBook.com

Follow God and Gigs on:
Facebook.com/godandgigs
Twitter.com/godandgigs
Instagram.com/godandgigs

© 2016 Allen C. Paul
All rights reserved.
For permission to share this information in any form, contact

## allenpaul@godandgigs.com

www.ingramcontent.com/pod-product-compliance
Lightning Source LLC
Chambersburg PA
CBHW052136010526
44113CB00036B/2279